Dear Ward & Patty,

Think it was an inspiration and
I felt it was an inspiration and
a beautiful lesson about loss and love.
With the gathering of family he can find
strength and especially at Christmas, we can
feel Gods love and abundance. flies given us the most
precious gift of all - his Son - Life everlasting. We can
live to fulfill our purpose here. There is never
enough time to being together forever beyond this life
And we can live to fulfill our purpose here. There is never
but through our fleeting time here, we can touch so many people there
without even realizing it and help, and love all those in need
is a lot of work to do but that may be something that makes a difference there
and an understanding of what is really important. We cannot hold her in
kiss her in touch her, our dear Roxy Lanie but like all those closer to the Lord
like the bending of light into a rainbow, it is always there, and We know....

We love you so very much

Merry Christmas 1994
Thelma & Jim
Genesis, Jimmy & Andrew

MERRY CHRISTMAS
With Love

This book is dedicated to my Grandma Grace Patty,
who once took a cherry pie to Old Lady Russell.

—S.P.

To my beloved wife Hilary, whose patience, wisdom, strength,
and humor enable me to accomplish the impossible.

—D.B.

Merry Christmas, With Love

Copyright © 1994 by Sandi Patty for text.
Copyright © 1994 by Doron Ben-Ami for illustrations.

Managing Editor: Laura Minchew
Project Editor: Brenda C. Ward

Library of Congress Cataloging-in-Publication Data

Patty, Sandi, 1956-
      Merry Christmas with love / by Sandi Patty ; illustrated by Doron Ben-Ami.
         p.   cm.
           "Word kids!"
Summary: Johnny can't understand why Old Mrs. Russell doesn't want him sledding in her yard, until one Christmas he finds out why she's so mean.
        ISBN 0-8499-1003-X :
[1. Christmas--Fiction.] I. Ben-Ami, Doron, ill. II. Title.
PZ7..P278155Me 1994
[E]--dc20

                               94-20487
                                  CIP
                                  AC

Printed in the United States of America
4 3 2 1 LBM 9 8 7 6 5 4 3 2 1

MERRY CHRISTMAS
With Love

by SANDI PATTY
ILLUSTRATED BY DORON BEN-AMI

WORD
kids!

WORD PUBLISHING
Dallas · London · Vancouver · Melbourne

Something drew her to the attic. She didn't know why;
she hadn't been up there in years . . . not since . . . well,
not in a very long time. As she fumbled to turn on the light,
she bumped a box and heard a Christmas bell jingle.

Christmas . . .

Leaning next to the Christmas box was the sled—
the red sled Billy got for Christmas so many years ago.
Oh, how his eyes had twinkled when he came down those stairs
that Christmas morning! He was twelve—so old, so young.

"Mom, this is the best Christmas ever! I love you, Mom. Thank you."

As she thought about that happy morning, she heard a noise that jarred her back to the present. She opened the attic window and yelled down at the boys in her yard.

"Johnny! How many times have I told you to keep that silly sled out of my yard. The next time you boys trespass in my yard, I'm gonna call your parents."

"We're sorry, Ol—uh, Mrs. Russell. We lost control of the sled. It won't happen again."

"It better not," she said and slammed shut the window.

"Old Lady Russell is such a hag," the boys began to complain, all except Johnny. There was something in the way Old Lady Russell looked at him. If she was so mean, why did she look so worried? Oh, well.

"See ya later, guys." Johnny picked up his red sled and went home.

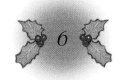

That evening Old Lady Russell (as the kids called her)
made some hot tea and a batch of cookies. She wasn't sure
why she did this. There wasn't anyone to share them with.
But it seemed like the thing to do. And for a moment,
good memories of times past brought a smile and comfort . . .
until, once again, the memory of what caused her sadness returned.

She took off her apron and felt something in the pocket.
Reaching in, she pulled out a small Christmas-tree ornament.
Where did this come from? Absent-mindedly she hung it on
a little plant in the corner. It was the closest thing to a
Christmas tree she'd had in years. As she turned out the light,
she heard herself saying, "Merry Christmas."
How long had it been since she'd said that?

8

School was out for Christmas vacation, and the neighborhood boys were taking turns with Johnny's sled. When it was Johnny's turn again, he dragged his sled up the hill then took off for the ride of his life. Unknown to him, Old Lady Russell saw it all. She saw the fear on his face when he realized the sled was out of control and the sheer delight when he crashed into a snowbank and was covered with snow from head to toe. She knew, too, that Johnny hadn't realized yet that he had landed directly in the middle of her yard. Old Lady Russell ran out onto her porch to see if Johnny was okay. Then, realizing she had let her guard down, she quickly scolded him.

"If I've told you once, I've told you a thousand times not to trespass in my yard! Come in this house at once, young man, and bring that silly red sled with you," she commanded.

Stunned and afraid, Johnny reluctantly followed Old Lady Russell into her house.

"You're Eddie Jones's son, aren't you?" she said. "He was my son's best friend."

ohnny remembered hearing his father talk about Billy's mom.
He said she was so nice, always making them cookies and treats.
Could this be the same lady? Old Lady Russell was anything but nice!

"I'm sorry to get in your yard," Johnny said. "I didn't mean any harm.
We were just playing, and I guess I was trying to go too fast."

"Take off your coat, young man, and hang it by the fire.
You'll catch your death of cold."

As Johnny put his coat by the fire, he noticed her pitiful
little plant in the corner with a Christmas ornament on it.
He also saw a faded picture on the mantle.

Sensing his question, she said, "That's my son, Billy.
He was about your age when he . . . when that picture was taken."

"How old are you, young man?" she asked.

"I'm twelve, ma'am."

Studying the picture, Johnny noticed that Billy also was covered with snow
from head to toe. He posed proudly with what looked like a brand-new sled.

"You boys don't like me much, do you?"

"It's not that we don't like you," he stuttered. "It's just that, . . .
well, it's . . . you seem kinda mad all the time."

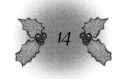

"Is that so? Come sit here and have some cookies and hot cocoa with me. I happen to know twelve-year-old boys like cookies and hot cocoa. I suppose you have big plans for Christmas."

"Oh yes, ma'am," he said with enthusiasm. "My brother's coming home from college, and we're gonna go chop our very own tree this year."

"That sounds nice," she said. And without realizing it, she added, "Christmas hasn't been the same for me for a long time."

"Will you be having Christmas with anyone this year, ma'am?"

She thought for a moment. How long had it been since she had shared Christmas with any friends or loved ones? She wanted to say she couldn't bear the memories. But all that came out was, "No, and quit being so nosy. Now, get your coat and run on home. And stay out of trouble."

"Yes, ma'am," Johnny said, scurrying for his coat, quite thankful to get out of there. "Thank you for the cookies."

"You're welcome, Johnny." On impulse, she quickly hugged him and said, "Please be careful, son. Now run on home."

As Johnny left, Mrs. Russell could not keep back the painful memories of that Christmas thirty years before. Her son, Billy, had been excited over the new red sled. He was so happy. "You're the greatest, Mom," said Billy. "Thanks. Wait 'til Eddie sees this. Wow! He won't believe it. Can I go over to his house? The snow is perfect."

"Sure you can," Mrs. Russell had said. Oh, how she loved to see her son happy. "Put your coat on and bundle up."

Then out the door he had gone with all of his contagious joy. He was in such a hurry he had tripped and stumbled down the porch steps. He was covered from head to toe with snow, and the two of them had shared a most precious giggle over the incident. "Wait right there," she had called, and ran to get her camera. "I want to remember this." After she snapped a quick photo, he had headed to Eddie's to show off his new red sled.

There had been such laughter all up and down the street that day. Out the kitchen window she had watched as Billy and Eddie took turns with the sled. It was Billy's turn again. He hiked up the hill, dragging his sled behind him. Then with complete abandon, he took off faster than he had ever gone before. But the sled kept going faster, and the delight on his face turned to panic and then to fear as the sled veered completely out of control. He couldn't stop it. Helplessly, she had watched as Billy's sled hit the big oak tree in front of Mrs. Turner's house.

"Wow, that was a good one," Eddie had shouted, running toward Billy.

"That's the best run I've ever seen. You okay, Bill? . . ."

But Billy didn't answer. He didn't even move. He just lay there.

"Come on, Billy. Stop kiddin' around. Get up."

Mrs. Russell had seen it all from her kitchen window, as had many of the neighbors. They all came running toward the big oak tree and Billy.

"Somebody get a doctor."

"Billy, get up. Please get up."

But Billy didn't get up. The doctor arrived, but all he could say was . . . "I'm so sorry. Billy broke his neck in the crash. I'm sure he didn't feel any pain."

For Mrs. Russell, it had been as if time were as frozen as the icicles on the houses. She was certain her own heart and her own breathing had stopped, too.

"Why? Oh dear God, why? My Billy was only twelve . . . so young."

Oh, how she missed him. How she longed just once more to make sure he had buttoned up his coat and tied his blue scarf around his neck before he went dashing off to school.

She thought of Johnny. What a sweet boy. He reminded her of Billy, red sled and all. She didn't want to let herself feel anything for him. But she knew it was too late. She actually allowed herself to hope—hope she might catch a glimpse of him tomorrow, Christmas Eve. Johnny didn't know it, but he had already brought a newness to her life.

Tomorrow, then, she thought. And for the first time in a long time, Mrs. Russell had a good night's sleep.

Johnny was quite shaken when he left Old Lady Russell's house. A lot of things seemed strange to him. If she was so mean, why did she offer him cookies? And that picture of her son—what was his name, Billy? He must remember to ask his dad more about Billy. And that plant with a Christmas ornament . . . was that all the Christmas decorations she had? Why did she say Christmas hadn't been the same for her? Johnny could not stop thinking about Mrs. Russell.

The next day was Christmas Eve. Johnny's brother finally came home from school, and they went to chop down their very own Christmas tree. What fun they had! They got home just in time for dinner. Johnny's mother asked him to change clothes because their family would be going to church for the Christmas Eve service. Then, after church, they would come home and decorate the tree.

Although Johnny had enjoyed chopping the tree with his brother, he was unusually quiet through dinner and now at church. His mind was on Mrs. Russell. What was she doing right now?

$\mathcal{P}$astor Johnson was talking.

"Jesus came to us as a baby," he began. "He was born, He lived, He died, and He rose again, all for us. He gave Himself—this is the greatest Christmas gift. And Jesus wants our gifts to be the same. Every gift must be given with a little bit of ourselves. To give yourself to someone is the greatest gift of all. Christmas is a time of joy for many people, but for others it is a time for loneliness, a reminder of their losses, their hurt, and their pain . . ."

That's it, Johnny thought. Loneliness. Mrs. Russell isn't mean; she's lonely. Suddenly, Johnny knew what he could do for her. As soon as church was over Johnny told his family about his experience with Old Lady Russell, how she scolded him, gave him cookies, and hugged him. He told them about the sad look in her eyes that he now knew was loneliness. "Pastor Johnson talked about giving ourselves to someone. I want to do something for Mrs. Russell."

$\mathcal{J}$ohnny's family caught his enthusiasm and his compassion
and began to put together a plan. "For starters," said his father,
"we can go see her. It's been a long time since
I've been in that house, not since Billy's accident."

He told his family the tragic events of that Christmas Day
so many years ago. They all sat quietly, each one teary-eyed,
until . . . finally, Johnny's mother suggested they take
Mrs. Russell some gifts when they went to visit.
"And how about a fresh cherry pie?" she added.

"And a Christmas tree," said Johnny. "She needs a
Christmas tree. But where could we get one tonight? . . ."
And then they all looked at the freshly cut evergreen
Johnny and his brother had so proudly brought home that day.

"That's perfect!" they all said. Then they hugged and laughed
and cried and did things people usually do when they are about to embark
on a most precious adventure called togetherness and caring.

26

Johnny's mother gathered up all the extra tree ornaments and lights. Johnny's dad and brother loaded the tree in the back of the station wagon, and Johnny grabbed the package with the new scarf he had carefully wrapped for his mother. He knew his mother would understand when he gave it to Mrs. Russell. Johnny had never felt like he felt that night. Maybe that was what Pastor Johnson meant when he had talked about giving yourself. Johnny was giving, and the joy in his heart was indescribable.

After what seemed like an eternity, they arrived at Mrs. Russell's house. On impulse, the four of them began to sing "Joy to the World" as they walked up her porch steps carrying the gifts, pie, and Christmas tree.

Mrs. Russell, startled at first by the singing, hurried to the front door. There, to her amazement, were Johnny and Eddie.

"Eddie, is that you?" She didn't know whether to laugh or cry or smile or hug or just what. So she did them all.

"Come in. Oh, do come in! Let me look at you. Oh, Eddie, I've missed you! You've grown into a fine young man." (She wondered to herself if he might look a bit like Billy would have looked all grown up.)

Eddie hugged her with tenderness and kissed her gently on the cheek. "I miss Billy, too. He was a good friend," said Eddie.

"This is my wife, Ann, and my son, Ronald. And I guess you know Johnny," he said with a twinkle in his eye.

While the others began to decorate the tree, Johnny gave Mrs. Russell the gift. "I hope you like it," said Johnny.

She opened the lovely scarf and gently tied it around her neck. "And I hope you like yours, too," she said as she bent down to get the knitting beside her.

"It's for you," she said as she tied the most beautiful blue scarf around Johnny's neck.

For Johnny and Mrs. Russell, it truly was the best Christmas ever . . .
because they each received and gave the greatest gift of all — love.